Look, a Jellyfish!

by Tessa Kenan

BUMBA BOOKS™

LERNER PUBLICATIONS ◆ MINNEAPOLIS

Note to Educators:

Throughout this book, you'll find critical thinking questions. These can be used to engage young readers in thinking critically about the topic and in using the text and photos to do so.

Lerner Publications Company
A division of Lerner Publishing Group, Inc.
241 First Avenue North
Minneapolis, MN 55401 USA

For reading levels and more information, look up this title at www.lernerbooks.com.

Library of Congress Cataloging-in-Publication Data

Names: Kenan, Tessa, author.
Title: Look, a jellyfish! / by Tessa Kenan.
Description: Minneapolis : Lerner Publications, [2017] | Series: Bumba books—I see ocean animals | Audience: Age 4–8. | Audience: K to Grade 3. | Includes bibliographical references and index.
Identifiers: LCCN 2016001252 (print) | LCCN 2016003142 (ebook) | ISBN 9781512414219 (lb : alk. paper) | ISBN 9781512415094 (pb : alk. paper) | ISBN 9781512415100 (eb pdf)
Subjects: LCSH: Jellyfishes—Juvenile literature.
Classification: LCC QL377.S4 K46 2017 (print) | LCC QL377.S4 (ebook) | DDC 593.5/3—dc23

LC record available at http://lccn.loc.gov/2016001252

Manufactured in the United States of America
1 – VP – 7/15/16

LERNER e SOURCE

Expand learning beyond the printed book. Download free, complementary educational resources for this book from our website, www.lernerresource.com.

Table of Contents

Jellyfish Float

Jellyfish are ocean animals.

There are many kinds.

They live in every ocean.

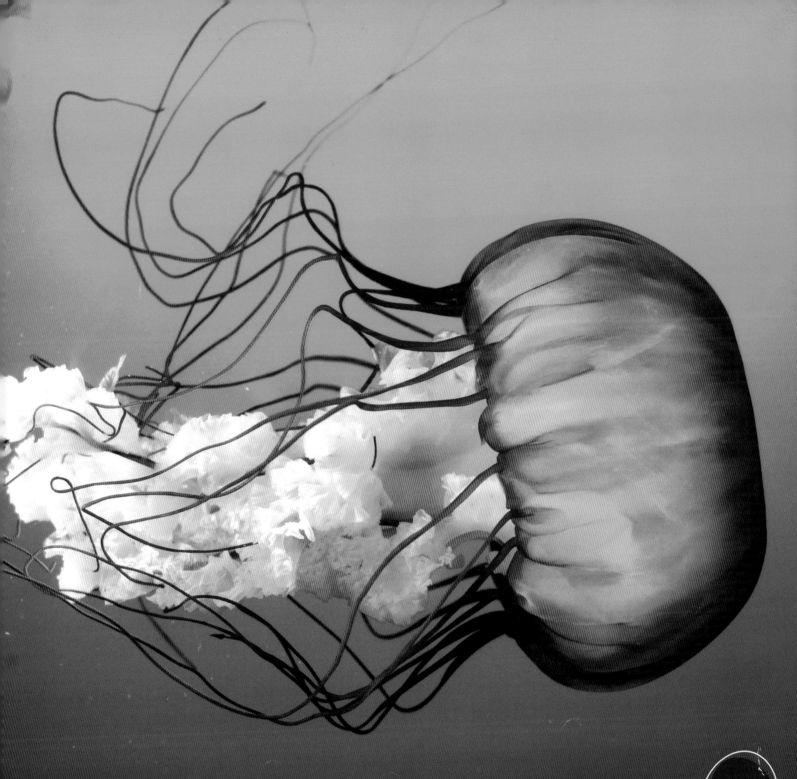

Some jellyfish

are orange.

Some are blue.

They can be many other

colors too.

Jellyfish have soft bodies.

They do not have bones.

Why might it be helpful to have soft bodies?

9

Long tentacles hang from jellyfish.

Jellyfish sting with these.

They sting their food.

Then they eat the food.

Why do you think jellyfish tentacles are long?

Jellyfish eat fish.

They eat plants.

They eat shrimp

and crabs.

The mouth is in the middle

of the body.

young jellyfish

Jellyfish lay eggs.

Young jellyfish live

on rocks.

Adult jellyfish swim.

The top of a jellyfish is called the bell.

A jellyfish can move its bell.

Moving the bell helps the jellyfish swim.

bell

A group of jellyfish is called

a bloom.

Jellyfish are light.

Water moves the bloom.

Some jellyfish can light up.

They light up when other animals touch them.

The light scares other animals away.

Why might animals be afraid of a jellyfish's light?

Parts of a Jellyfish

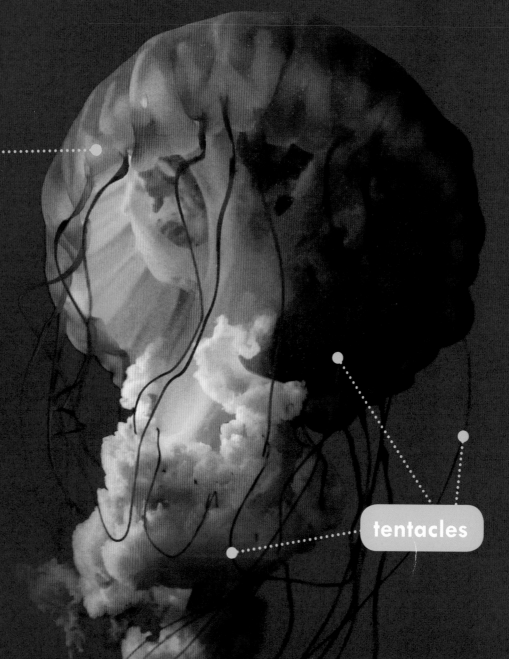

bell

tentacles

Picture Glossary

bell

the top of
a jellyfish

bloom

a group of jellyfish

light up

to shine in the dark

tentacles

long, thin arms
that hang from
an animal's body

23

Index

Read More

Gibbs, Maddie. *Jellyfish*. New York: PowerKids Press, 2014.

Hansen, Grace. *Jellyfish*. Minneapolis: Abdo Publishing, 2015.

Meister, Cari. *Jellyfish*. Minneapolis: Bullfrog Books, 2015.

Photo Credits